The Land of CHINA

Lynn M. Stone

The Rourke Book Company, Inc.
Vero Beach, Florida 32964

© 2001 The Rourke Book Company, Inc.

PHOTO CREDITS
© Lynn M. Stone: title page, p. 21; © Keren Su: p. 4, 7, 8,
10, 12, 13, 15, 17, 18

Library of Congress Cataloging-in-Publication Data

Stone, Lynn M.
   The land of China / Lynn M. Stone.
      p. cm. — (China)
   Includes index.
   ISBN 1-55916-318-6
   1. China—Juvenile literature. [1. China] I. Title.

DS706 .S794 2000
951—dc21
                                        00–038724

Printed in the USA

CONTENTS

THE LAND OF CHINA

Almost everyone has seen pictures of crowded cities in China. People seem to be everywhere!

It is true: China has more than 1 billion people, more than any other nation. But China is the world's third-largest country in area. The land of China is far more than one crowded city after another. In fact, most Chinese people live in the eastern one-third of the country.

Beyond the cities, China has natural beauty, like the hills of Guangxi.

China stretches some 3,000 miles (4,800 kilometers) from east to west. That's about the distance from New York to Los Angeles. With so much territory, China has a rich mix of land types and **climates**. Beyond China's busy cities are great plains, mountains, valleys, lakes, **deserts**, forests, and over 4,000 miles (6,400 kilometers) of seashore.

A horseman stands at the shore of Heaven Lake in Xinjiang along the ancient trade route called the Silk Road.

THE MOUNTAINS

Much of China's **terrain** is hilly or mountainous. China has several major mountain ranges. The Himalayas in the west are the highest mountains in the world. One Himalayan peak, snowy Mount Everest, is the world's tallest mountain. It stands about 29,000 feet (8,840 meters) above sea level.

China's Tian Shan mountain range has peaks over 20,000 feet (6,096 meters). The Qin Ling Mountains are 12,000 feet (3,658 meters) high.

The grand Himalayas in western China are the world's tallest peaks.

The Qin Ling Mountains form a very important natural wall, east to west, across China. The Qin Lings block winds and clouds. That results in two very different types of land on either side of the mountains.

Chinese farmers grow wheat in the dry climate north of the mountains. They grow rice in the damp climate south of the mountains.

Chinese farmers in the dry area north of the Qin Ling Mountains grow rich crops of wheat.

Farmers in Xinjiang raise sheep in dry grasslands.

The Himalayas of Tibet glow in early morning light.

13

DESERTS

China's Taklimakan Desert in the northwest part of the country is one of the driest deserts in the world. Near it lies the Turpan Depression. At 505 feet (154 meters) below sea level it is the lowest point in China.

The Ordos, Alxa, and Gobi Deserts are in eastern China. Unlike China's cities, the deserts have few people.

The Taklimakan Desert here in Xinjiang, along the Silk Road route, is one of several deserts In China.

RIVERS

Among China's rivers are two of the largest in the world. They are the Yangtze River and the Huang He, or Yellow River.

The Yangtze is the fourth-longest river in the world. Some of China's best farmland is in the Yangtze River valley.

The Yellow River long ago earned the nickname "China's Sorrow." It flooded villages in its valley and drowned thousands of people. Dams and canals prevent major flooding now.

The Daning River has cut through rock on its rush to join the Yangtze.

FORESTS AND PLANTS

China has a broad mix of climates and land types. That has given the country a wide range of plants.

The plant life of China is not completely unlike the plant life of North America. But China has lost much of its forest cover to woodcutting.

Tropical coconut trees grow along the beach by the South China Sea.

Moist eastern China has richer plant life than drier western China. Tropical rain forests and **mangrove** swamps are in the southeast. Elsewhere in the east, China has forests of evergreens and broad-leafed plants.

In China, just as in North America, you could see such familiar trees as pine, birch, oak, and spruce. But you might also see thickets of wild bamboo in China.

Part of China, like the American West, is covered by grassland, or **prairie**.

Moist, mountain forests are the homes of China's rare giant pandas.

CHINA'S CLIMATE

Climate is the long-term weather of a place. China has a broad range of climates because of its great size. Climates vary from wet and warm to bitterly cold in Tibet and northern Manchuria.

In certain desert areas, summer temperatures top 100 degrees Fahrenheit (38 degrees Celsius). On winter nights, desert temperatures may dip to 30 degrees below zero Fahrenheit (-34 degrees Celsius).

Southeast China has storms called **monsoons** each summer or autumn. Monsoons are similar to North America's hurricanes.

GLOSSARY

climate (KLIE mut) — the long-term temperature and moisture levels of a location; weather

desert (DE zert) — a region, hot or cold, with little total rainfall or snowfall each year

mangrove (MAN growv) — a type of bushy tree that grows in salt water in tropical regions

monsoon (MAHN SOON) — a series of hurricane-like storms during summer or fall in southeast Asia

prairie (PRAIR ee) — a grassland

terrain (ter RAYN) — the physical features of a piece of land

FURTHER INFORMATION

Find out more about the land of China and China in general with these helpful books and information sites:

- Field, Catherine. *China*. Raintree Steck-Vaughn, 2000
- Weterlow, Julia. *China*. Franklin Watts, 1996

China on-line at www.mytravelguide.com

Lonely Planet-Destination China on-line at www.lonelyplanet.com

INDEX